P9-BMI-991

D0426339

Presented to:

....

From:

....

Date:

....

dear daughters

love letters to the
next generation

SUSIE DAVIS

Abingdon Press

Growing in Life, Serving in Faith

NASHVILLE

DEAR DAUGHTERS

LOVE LETTERS TO THE NEXT GENERATION

Copyright © 2019 by Abingdon Press

All rights reserved.

No part of this work may be reproduced or transmitted in any form or by any means, electronic or mechanical, including photocopying and recording, or by any information storage or retrieval system, except as may be expressly permitted by the 1976 Copyright Act or in writing from the publisher. Requests for permission can be addressed to Permissions, The United Methodist Publishing House, 2222 Rosa L. Parks Blvd., Nashville, TN, 37228-1306 or emailed to permissions@umpublishing.org.

Library of Congress Cataloging-in-Publication Data has been requested

ISBN-13 978-1-5018-8106-0

Scripture quotations marked ESV are from the ESV® Bible (The Holy Bible, English Standard Version®), copyright © 2001 by Crossway, a publishing ministry of Good New Publishers. Used by permission. All rights reserved.

Scripture quotations marked (GNT) are from the Good New Translation in Today's English Version-Second Edition © 1992 by American Bible Society. Used by permission.

Scripture quotations marked NASB are taken from the New American Standard Bible® (NASB), Copyright © 1960, 1962, 1963, 1968, 1971, 1972, 1973, 1975, 1977, 1995 by The Lockman Foundation. Used by permission. www.Lockman.org

Scripture quotations marked (NIV) are taken from the Holy Bible, New International Version®, NIV®. Copyright © 1973, 1978, 1984, 2011 by Biblica, Inc.™ Used by permission of Zondervan. All rights reserved worldwide. www.zondervan.com The "NIV" and "New International Version" are trademarks registered in the United States Patent and Trademark Office by Biblica, Inc.™

Scripture quotations marked (NLT) are taken from the Holy Bible, New Living Translation, copyright © 1996, 2004, 2015 by Tyndale House Foundation. Used by permission of Tyndale House Publishers, Inc., Carol Stream, Illinois 60188. All rights reserved.

19 20 21 22 23 24 25 26 27—10 9 8 7 6 5 4 3 2 1

MANUFACTURED IN THE PEOPLE'S REPUBLIC OF CHINA

Dedication

To my mother.

*The kindest, gentlest woman I've
ever known, who showed me what
it means to be a loving mother.*

Contents

Foreword

You and I are really so lucky Susie wrote this book you're holding. I'll probably end up carrying a beat-up copy in my back pocket for myself and extra copies for all the women I know who desperately need someone to pour into their life. I've already dusted off a little spot on my bookshelf, right next to my other favorite book, *A Gift from the Sea*. Susie and I both love *A Gift from the Sea*, written long ago by Anne Morrow Lindbergh, as a look at the life of a modern woman. It's a book that's always mentored me as I go about my own days looking to live deeply and wholely.

When Susie and I met in 2011, I couldn't know it then, but it would change my life forever. Our relationship started routinely enough. One day, my inbox dinged with an email from Susie, someone a bit younger than my own mom. We'd never met, but she wondered if I'd work with her on a web-design project. Susie probably wasn't looking to forge a long-lasting relationship with me; she was just trying to get work finished. I *know* Susie wasn't planning on becoming a spiritual mama to me, but I was hungry for her leadership and love.

The thing about Susie is that her eyes are always, always open to what God is doing in her midst. She pays attention. She asks *the best* questions. She's genuinely curious about people.

I remember when we finished that web-design project, she sent me a candle from Anthropologie as a thank you. What a delight! I felt specially and personally thought of, and I was grateful.

Over the years, I somehow became a dear daughter of hers, and she acts as a spiritual mom I've never had. I'm not really sure exactly how that happened, and if you know Susie you know *everyone* asks me how I managed to pull it off. Life is a mystery! I think I asked her to spend time with me routinely over the phone and be a mentor of sorts. Like I said, I was hungry and thirsty to be invested in. Eventually I was in a very difficult season and I invited myself to Austin, and we met in real life for the first time. She picked me up at the airport in her cute car, with her cute self ready with the kindest, most welcoming hug, and all the fun, quirky plans. We are quite a pair. We visited art shops and talked about pie making. She let me sleep in, she took me out to dinner. That weekend, I felt mothered in such a restorative way.

Susie was the first person who uttered the words "You'll probably write a book someday" to me, and that off-the-cuff statement was wisely and quickly followed up with "but, you have so much time. Please, don't rush into it." She has quietly pushed napkins toward me to dry my sloppy tears at happy hour. She's counseled me in tough church situations and difficulties with my dad.

There's at least one story about Susie in all my books, because Susie asks me questions that cause me to dig deep into myself and even deeper into God. She's not afraid to ask questions for which you might not know the answer. She's a delightful gift whose wisdom shifts eternity for me.

I've always wanted to duplicate Susie a couple hundred times so she could be all these wonderful things to *everyone* I meet. I have an embarrassment of riches in her care! I haven't quite figured out the duplication technology, but here in this book is something just about as great…It's Susie's heart for you, her words.

We all long to be mothered. This deep and profound need does not cease to exist when we are eighteen years old and graduated high school. In fact, getting married, having babies, choosing a lane professionally, these are all times of life that can knock us off our axis and challenge what we know to be true. Losing parents, losing jobs, making and losing friends, these are times where the comfort, wisdom, and strength of a mother can help sturdy us and help us grow. Not everyone's biological or parental mother has the time, ability, or desire to be engaged in our life beyond our childhood, but we still need mother figures to help nurture us through adulthood.

Did you know Susie takes notes when we talk, most every time? It's slightly unnerving and the most endearing thing. I'm thankful someone cares enough to find something about me notable in some small way. She's loving me by noticing me.

Since you've got this book, which is the next best thing to sitting across from Susie, you may as well get your journal out, too. You're going to want to take notes. Write down every question she asks, and take the time to answer. She's helping you notice yourself, and she's helping you notice God. These questions will change the way you view the world, and help you believe better.

You're holding the heart of the wisest, kindest woman I know. Her heart for you is huge. It's filled with homemade pie and Texas-sized bouquets and mystery and whimsy and wonder. She will make you believe more is possible of your life, of God, and also that you have so much time to experience it all. She'll make you hopeful, but never rushed. She'll challenge you to look within, and to look ahead. She's masterful in the way she loves gently and completely, and this book is a book of wisdom for modern women.

I cannot wait to share Susie with you, as her own real-life daughters have shared her with me!

Hayley Morgan

dear daughters

Introduction

For over a decade, younger women clustered around me like hummingbirds to purple salvia. Swooping into my life for a season, gathering fuel to live a purposeful and spiritual life. I had no idea way back then why I should be graced by this charm; I only knew they peered attentively at me over my kitchen counter. They spilled open their hearts, all honest and vulnerable, while I soaped up dishes. Some sat at my dining room table eating Sunday supper with my family, tucked in beside us as our own. Others joined us on family trips.

These girls often called or texted me. Some even Skyped and FaceTimed. Over the years, we've met together in small groups for Bible study or book clubs. We've attended cooking classes together and gone on writing retreats. We've taken small-town excursions, planted flowers in my front yard, and had happy hour on my back patio. Year in and year out, no matter the season, it seemed that there was always a younger woman by my side. It was natural, organic. And they were all looking for the same thing: the nectar of age and wisdom that only an older woman provides. Who knew nectar was sourced from a forty-something-year-old woman whose face was etched with expression lines and whose life carried a long history of learning things the hard way with God?

This mentoring of young women started when my oldest child, Will (now in his early thirties), was a senior in high school. Four of his friends asked me if I would lead them in a Bible study. They sensed the big transition from high school to college had the opportunity to knock them off balance and they wanted an "older woman" to teach them how to move gracefully from one season to the next.

The mentoring opportunity happened again when I was on a class trip abroad with my second child, Emily (now in her late twenties), during her senior year in high school. In the absence of having their own moms on the trip, Emily's friends and peers cloistered around me when they needed a mother figure. It was actually on that trip that the girls started calling me Mama Suz—an endearing term they created meant to offer respect coupled with fond familiarity.

By the time my youngest child, Sara (now in her midtwenties), entered college, Mama Suz was the way all my kids introduced me to their friends. I was firmly established as a mother figure. Someone my own children would refer their friends to in seasons of confusion or grief. Someone ready to take a call, meet over coffee, or serve up a home-cooked meal.

Then the mentor opportunities started happening online. Young women I never met in person reached out to me on social media, asking for guidance and wisdom. At ministry events, girls sought me out, thanking me for encouraging them through my short open-letter posts written for my daughters on Instagram, Facebook, and my blog.

Though I didn't know it then, I was fulfilling a call on my life. Through my mothering, I was doing the good things God planned for me long ago.[1]

Yep, simply by opening my heart and making room for more than just my children, I was fulfilling a great commission on my life, participating in a special ministry that God fashioned for me[2]—to encourage the dear daughters in my world to love God body, heart, and mind in their unique situations. To train young women to be strengthened in the inner being.[3]

After over a decade of being available to mother the young people in my proximity and beyond, I have discovered God's specific ministry plan for me: to boldly encourage and lead dear daughters. And this is the simple way I do it: by being a spiritual mama.

It's not complicated. It doesn't require a degree in counseling or theology. It just means I stay authentically connected to Jesus. It means I am doggedly determined to maintain and remember my identity as an "older woman." Not someone looking to be popular or hip or eternally young; rather a woman who is sober to the ways of the Spirit. Enthused and identified with the things of God. Someone who does not let her own struggles and disappointments get in the way of her children's best interest. This is my heart for the dear daughters God brings me. As long as there are young women in need of spiritual guidance, I will be a minister of the gospel. But even more: I will be a spiritual mother.

Though I struggled when my own children left the nest, I have realized this amazing truth: a woman never need have an empty nest. And so, a mother's job is never over.

The world is full of dear daughters who need a godly woman a few steps ahead. They need someone to help them navigate life as a young woman in all the seasons of life: during college, starting a new job, marrying a man, becoming a mother.

I know this because I remember being a young woman.

I've been journaling, tracking my heart and spirit, since I was fourteen years old. Writing out my thoughts and prayers, chronicling life without realizing it. A few weeks ago, I found a big stash of old journals and read through a few of them. Inside the pages, I could see this woman I used to be. The struggles, the joys—all things laid bare on the page. Completely naked by paper and pen. Vulnerable.

I wanted to hug her and tell her the things she prayed over so ferociously would all be okay. I wanted to hand her a cup of hot tea and tell her to settle her heart and enjoy those ridiculously simple moments being a mom. I wanted to tell her things would work out. That God was always taking care.

I would have handed her this book. I would have offered to read it with her. Because this book is a love letter about life. A reminder of God's presence and love and wonder in the middle of our everything.

There are so many dear daughters in the world who need a hand and a heart to follow. The world needs more spiritual mamas. Older, godly women who realize that mothering is a sacred trust from God. Women who gratefully acknowledge age and experience in order to lead a younger generation. Women who embrace the fact that mothering is a celebration of life and goodness and God.

We need to have these conversations together, one by one, and celebrate what it looks like to embrace the simplicity and beauty of being a godly woman.

Chapter One:

On Worry

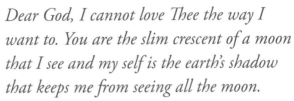

On Worry

Dear God, I cannot love Thee the way I want to. You are the slim crescent of a moon that I see and my self is the earth's shadow that keeps me from seeing all the moon.
— Flannery O'Connor

*g*od woke the sun this morning. Same as every morning. He merely whispered and the sun rose, gently pulling golden pink clouds across the pale sky. The moon quietly faded away, winking at me as she went. She'll be back later tonight in the very same spot, hovering happily against a milky black canvas spotted with stars.

I watch this transition daily from my back patio. It is such a comfort to me to see the familiar routine. Sun and moon, moon and sun. There they are in the big Texas sky, little dime-shaped discs to my eyes, moving slowly into place. The interchange is seamless, like God is playing checkers in the sky, though I know the reality is more like a massive, cosmic dance. Isn't it beautiful that God is in control of the sun, the moon, and the stars? And even better, he's in control of you and me too.

I wouldn't have believed that if you told me when I was a teenager. Because something happened that was so traumatic, it robbed me of belief that God holds the world in his hands.

I was a fourteen-year-old girl sitting in my English classroom, listening as my teacher spoke, when suddenly my classmate, a neighbor boy whom I had known for years, walked in with a rifle and shot and killed my teacher. My life dramatically changed that day and my view of God along with it.

Though I heard about Jesus two years earlier at a Young Life camp and had developed a deep love for God, after the murder I started to distrust him. I felt like he must have forgotten those of us in that classroom that day: he must have been somewhere on the other side of the world, managing something more important, like the daily interchange of the sun, moon, and stars.

In the years that followed, anxiety crept into my life, infiltrating the tiniest spaces. I worried about bad, violent things happening again, but I also worried about small things. Because after the murder, I felt God was far too busy managing bigger things to keep thoughtful watch over me. So I started taking care of myself, doing anything and everything to keep bad things from happening by my own power.

White-knuckling my life that way soon developed into a joy-crushing stronghold of fear. Because even as I frantically tried to keep my life stable and beautiful, I knew that I was powerless to stop unexpected things from surprising and astounding and saddening me once again.

I know you, too, have experienced things that make you feel anxious. It doesn't have to be something as shocking as a murder: It's not just the big things that take us by surprise.

It's the small and middle-sized things too. The job loss, the totaled car, or the misunderstanding between you and your friend. Maybe it's the inability to get pregnant, the wrecked relationship with your dad, or the ongoing tension between you and your mom. Things no one else would label as catastrophic, but things that break your heart apart bit by bit just the same.

It's easy to move into autopilot when hard things happen. We get by. We cope. We push past the disappointments and keep living life. But then days, months, or even years later, we're trying to deal with unexplained and ongoing tension, completely unaware of its origin. Because we've become accustomed to dismissing the heartache over and over, rather than honestly looking at the bigger issue of disappointment with God.

For example, I recently got a letter from a dear daughter. And I want to share a little bit of it,

because it's a small peek into an honest heart dealing with the same minor catastrophes we all face. She wrote:

I read your post (on social media) about loving God but not trusting him. I grew up in a Christian home and my parents were divorced when I was twelve years old. I love God but don't trust him with my heart. As I see friend after friend get divorced, I wonder if I'm next. I'm full of anxiety and fear and have been for years, and it won't go away. It's taking over my life. I don't know what to do. How did you stop worrying?

I love how she gets right to it. First, she identifies her heartbreak: the divorce of her parents when she was twelve years old. Second, she identifies the coping technique: fear. And then she throws out the question: How did you stop worrying?

I stopped worrying because my worry broke me down. I was a young

If you are bound up in anxiety, you'll miss the daily wonder. How God has filled the world to the brim with curious beauty. How he whispers to the sun and it rises. Let him whisper to you too.

mom with a baby boy who literally felt like everything was on her shoulders. I constantly thought about the next awful thing that might happen if I wasn't hyperalert and always on guard. I felt wholly responsible for everything in his life, even the things I couldn't control. It was exhausting. Our small shoulders are not meant to carry that kind of pressure. So I cratered and God caught me.

I don't want you to have to go through a breakdown, though if you do, God does have a way of coming through most miraculously and magnificently. But what if you pretend I'm sitting right there with you and we poke around a little about when all the worrying started for you?

What was it in your life that prompted the anxious thoughts? Sit for a minute and ask God to help you remember. And then honest as you're able, think on how you might be using coping techniques to handle some heartbreak between you and God.

Thinking things are one way and

seeing how quickly things change can make us want to take a stranglehold on life. But no matter how tightly we hold on, it doesn't mean we can control outcomes.

When I think back on witnessing the murder now, I realize the hardest thing to get over was this idea that God wasn't as big and trustworthy and helpful as I originally thought. And that maybe he didn't love me enough to step in and intervene. That's when I decided to micromanage my life as a coping technique.

What about you? How has your heart been broken? How did you take over?

So many dear daughters I talk with diminish their pain by either trying not to think about the original issues or by sweeping them away. What if instead you looked with compassion and curiosity about the source of the problem and heartbreak it created?

When you speak up about the problem and identify the unsuccessful ways you're addressing them, that's when you can really get help. What is your honest feeling toward God? Do you really trust him? Or has there been something that causes you to withhold yourself from him? Is there something that creates an uneasiness and pushes you toward managing things on your own?

The problem with all the worry is that it blinds you of the wonder. The wonder you experience when you lie on your back and watch white clouds float by against the blue sky. The wonder of the how it feels to stand outside in the cool grass and sip in the summer air without those nagging thoughts filling up your head. I think now that some of those early first moments being a new mom were wrecked because instead of marveling at the bundle of wonder before me, I was worrying about what to do next.

Annie Dillard writes, "Every day has its own particular brand of holiness to discover and worship appropriately."

I agree.

I know this from experience: if you are bound up in anxiety, you'll miss the daily wonder. How God has filled the world to the brim with curious beauty. How he whispers to the sun and it rises. Let him whisper to you too.

I want you to be open to your one beautiful life. Because you and I only get one, right? So we walk forward into the unexpected, pain and all. We walk forward in faith, though at times limping, knowing that God is still there for us.

We take tiny, brave steps forward today. No thinking about tomorrow's problems or next week's issues. Just for today, think only on today.

Maybe your one brave step today means today you make an appointment to meet with a counselor. Or today, you set aside something that you can't control, that you have obsessed over fixing. Or today, you take a break from watching all the horrifying negative news that's freaking you out and helping absolutely no one.

How will you practice peace today? Just today. Not tomorrow or next week. Speak it out, write it out, get it out.

You know the very good news? As you practice that one thing, for just today, you are actively loving and trusting God. And all we can really ever do is love God today. In this one moment, loving and trusting, pushing aside fear and worry.

Just as the sun and moon surrender daily to God's hand, I'm praying you find that small space to surrender your heart to God.

dear daughters

Susie Davis

Chapter Two:

On Life's Purpose

Chapter Two:

On Life's Purpose

It is very important to realize that our vocation is hidden in where we are and who we are.

— Henri Nouwen

It's 5:00 am. I open my eyes, stretch my arms overhead and look out the shadeless window. The moon's glow streams through the branches of the three-hundred-year-old live oak tree just outside. It's like my very own stained glass window. I sit up and look across the bedroom floor at the complex, shadowed pattern of tree limbs and moonlight. All is quiet except for a lone nightjar singing in the dark.

Since moving to our house beside the creek a year ago, we've adjusted to lots of new sounds. The loud buzzing of the cicadas on a hot summer's night, the tiny little frogs living under my potted plants whose chirps sound just

like a small bird's. And then there are
the bullfrogs. They blurt out songs to
each other at dusk. My husband, Will,
and I joke that it sounds like a bar
filled with old men who are drinking
too much and laughing too loudly.
Down at the creek leading up to the
greenbelt, we also hear owls hoot,
hawks screech, and even ducks call.
But what really caught our attention
was the Chuck-will's-widow.

In early summer, when the moon
is finding her place in the sky, that's
when the Chuck-will's-widow starts to
cry. It's musical and mystical. Sounds a
bit melancholy, almost like the bird is
calling out in uncertainty.

Upon hearing the unique cry at
night, I researched the species. The
Chuck-will's-widow is the largest
nightjar in North America and is often
mistaken for its famous cousin, the
Whip-poor-will. Both birds have a
distinct song that sounds like a forlorn
kind of cry. Neither of the birds builds
a nest, but instead they lay their eggs
on the open ground. It's hard not to

feel a little angst for a bird that stays up all night crying and has no nest to call home.

I had the exact same feeling recently after meeting with a dear daughter who wanted to talk about her life. More specifically, she wanted to know how to discover what she's supposed to do with her life, vocationally. She talked, she cried, and all she really wanted was for God to somehow handwrite her a list of instructions for the future. But, of course, that didn't happen—doesn't happen—so she met with me and wondered out loud over and over: What am I supposed to do with my life?

Honestly, I think this is the question I get most often from women, whether they're twenty years old or fifty years old. They just want to know what they're supposed to do with their time and energy. What kind of jobs, what kind of day-to-day activities will bring them in line with God's purpose for their lives?

Maybe you wonder about that too?

And maybe you feel a little like that nightjar, calling out to God every night in your prayers: What am I supposed to do with this one life?

I certainly struggled with that, especially in my early twenties. While I might look centered in my life purpose now, I'll let you in on a little something: I changed my major in college no less than ten times. Not only that, I attended five colleges. Five! When I finally graduated, over four years after I started, I graduated with thirty or so hours that I didn't actually need, meaning I took class after class that didn't end up mattering for my major or my future. My summary statement regarding school is this: I had no idea what I was supposed to do with my life. And at that point, I was totally fine with it. I'm glad my dad was okay with it, too, since he was the one paying for all those extra hours.

I think those unneeded classes reflected the fact that I was trying to figure out my life purpose. And at twenty years old, it just wasn't clear yet. Unless you know you want to be a doctor or something, it's actually kind of crazy to expect that young people, upon finishing high school or even college, should know what in the world they're supposed to do with the next four to five decades of their life. Our system seems a little flawed in that way. So, permission granted to be a twenty-year-old who's a little confused about your vocation. You're not alone.

And permission to be continually confused if, after college, you still wonder if you're "doing what you're supposed to be doing." Because no matter your age, it's easy to intermix your life purpose—or identity— with your vocation. They often are entangled, but they are unique and different. One is about your God-gifted value, and that has nothing to do with work. It has to do with your personality, your passion, and your preferences. The other is about your vocational expression of those things.

For many women, me included, the

*A*ll she really wanted was for God to somehow handwrite her a list of instructions for the future. But, of course, that didn't happen—doesn't happen—so she met with me and wondered out loud over and over: What am I supposed to do with my life?

two get so interwoven that they seem like one big thing. Like the way the big ole branches on our live oak are so sizeable they could be mistaken for the trunk. But they're not; they're an extension of the trunk. In the same way, who you are and what you do are intertwined, but understanding their distinctions will make you feel a lot less pressure and give you a ton of understanding.

So let's separate them out. Identity is who you are. And who you are is what defines you and your worth. You are made in the image of God. You are unique. There is no one like you. That uniqueness includes your gifting, your personality, your skill set. God crafted you with his design in mind. You were made by God and for God.[4] And you are called to be a minister to God and others. That is who you are. That is your life purpose.

The vocation part is your work and what you choose to do with your time, and there's a lot of wiggle room inside that. I think most people, during the course of their lives, do a lot of different things vocationally. For me, I can think of about ten jobs I've had between the ages of twenty and fifty. I've been a preschool teacher, a drama instructor, a public speaker, an author, a radio co-host. I've created small businesses that generated income to help with our family budget.

Vocationally, I've been all over the map. If I defined my worth or identity by my ability to stay the course doing one thing vocationally or by making big money, I'd feel like a colossal failure. Instead, I stay focused on my identity before God. I am made by him and for him, and in all the things I've chosen to do, I try to honor him.

Theologian Richard Foster says it like this: "My whole life, in one sense, has been an experiment in how to be a portable sanctuary, learning to practice the presence of God."[5]

Everywhere you go, as you practice the presence of God in your lives, you're like a small sanctuary to the people closest by. So that means when you're on the way to work and you interact with the barista in the morning, you're standing there as a respite. Giving life and comfort to the person you're talking to.

Or maybe as you hold your infant, or read to your toddler, you're offering them sanctuary as you abide with God. Maybe in your high pressure job with people who don't know or maybe even care about God, there you are, a portable sanctuary. A daily relief. It's that simple.

A lot of times, I think we try to make this connection between our identity and our vocation too intense and difficult. Like maybe being a minister for God always means you have to pack up your life and move to a third-world country to be a missionary. And you could be called to that, and it would be dreamy and romantic in a sacrificial kind of way. But more likely, your ministry to God is just right where you are, in your home and at your work.

That means if you are a first grade
teacher, your vocation is teaching. You
teach because you love it, hopefully,
but let's be gut level honest too: you
teach because they pay you. You have
bills to pay, and you happen to be
good with kids, so that's what you do.

But let's also look at how your
identity, as a child of God, is
enmeshed in your job. It's Monday
morning. You're tired but you get
up, meet with God, and while you're
praying, you're thinking of your
students, so you pray for them,
too. They are tiny and needy and
sometimes exhausting, but you love
them. You want a lot for them. Yes,
you'd like to teach them all to read
and write, but you'd also love for them
to know they are loved regardless
of academic performance. So when
you get to school, no matter how
exhausting your day may be, you keep
that goal in mind: to let your students
see God's unconditional love through
you. And that right there is a reflection
of your identity. You know you are

made by God and for God, and you
want to be a sanctuary.

I want you to sense the value of
what you do. Whatever you do. It's
my prayer actually, right out of the
Bible, that no matter what you do,
you always "sense the worth of your
work."[6]

That is important and dignifying.
But I don't want you to get confused
in thinking that you're only valuable
if you produce something and have
a big, important, meaningful job.
Because while that is the way society
thinks, it's not the way God thinks.

Your worth is assigned by God.
There is no job that can make you
more or less valuable in his eyes. And
as a side note, that's why we treat
everyone the same no matter their
job, position, or social standing. The
principal, the lead teacher, the new
teacher, the custodian, the child—all
are assigned deep, unconditional worth
and love from God.

So back to you. Here are a few
questions to help you sort things out.

How do you make money? Are you happy with that situation? Never mind how much money: If it's enough to live on, do you find joy there? Is it suited well to your personality and your skill set?

Who are you in God? List some words that you think God would use to describe you. Then check them out biblically to see if those are your words for you or God's words for you.

And finally, how do you differentiate between your job and your identity? Because there is a big difference. And it might be the very thing that keeps you from the haunting question: What am I supposed to do with my life?

Sometimes you might feel like a nightjar singing out all lonely in the night, wondering what to do and who you are, and I get that because I've had those seasons too. But you need to know that God hears you; he's not irritated by you, and he has good plans for you.

And one other thing, dear daughter: I'm praying for you. I'm praying that God will give you complete knowledge of his will and spiritual wisdom and understanding. And that the way you live will always honor him. And that you'll grow to know him better and better.[7]

I love you. Amen.

dear daughters

Susie Davis

Chapter Three:

On Loving
Your Body

Chapter Three:

On Loving Your Body

Pretty women wonder where my secret lies.
— Maya Angelou

anging just outside my patio window by my bedroom is a fabulous white vintage birdcage I bought at an estate sale. On hot summer nights at dusk, I love filling the cage with as many small votive candles as it can hold. Then I put on my bathing suit, grab a towel and scatter bath salts in the outdoor tub as it slowly fills with water. Finally, I sink my body into that bathtub, candlelight glistening overhead, and listen to the cicadas sing their summer song.

I remember one night in particular, I lay there and observed my body. I thought about the journey we'd seen. I thanked God for the five-plus decades of good, hard work my body had provided. Besides the everyday living and breathing and getting to do a lot of things I really love, like horseback riding, this body of mine also birthed three of the people I love most in the world. Which is a miracle and all brilliance on God's part.

Then to be completely truthful, I also gave thanks for the vintage tub because I was grateful to have my own little private pool to sink into—without having to deal with the inevitable internal drama of getting my fifty-something-year-old body to a public pool in a bathing suit.

I wondered on this paradox: the fact that I am okay with my body when it's just me and my body, but add in a handful of people and me standing there in a bathing suit, and suddenly I've got a little angry devil on my shoulder whispering all kinds of hateful things about my body. But, of course, on my other shoulder is the kind, affirming angel. Both voices in my head, chattering away. I'd like to say the unfriendly voice started after having babies. That my inner dialogue was created by the wear and tear of the three pregnancies and three C-sections that resulted in all the stretch marks and scars. But it started so much earlier.

I remember summers spent at the neighborhood pool when I was grade-school age, becoming aware of the roundness of my stomach compared to the leaner stomachs of a few of my friends. (Thinking back, swimsuits and pool time must have instigated much of my inner dialogue.) Then the summer after seventh grade, when my friends and I started wearing bikinis, the internal smack-talk really accelerated because some of my friends looked sixteen while I still looked about twelve. It was awkward waiting for my body to figure out how to grow up. By seventeen, it was a full-out body comparison. I was on the cheerleading team in high school, and every day we would weigh-in in front of each other. That's so smart, right?

Gathering a bunch of high school girls in a small room with a large standing scale as judge. Why did we do that? I guess it was inevitable, though, the weird ways we come to start judging our bodies, whether alone or in groups. Or even the way the scale measures our worthiness. I've never met a dear daughter who hasn't had a similar experience.

What about you? When did you start looking in the mirror and mentally questioning the goodness of what looks back at you? When did you stop believing you were fearfully and wonderfully made? I think we can blame a ton of this on the tsunami-sized load of communication about what the "ideal" female body looks like. Just turn on the TV or go online, and you'll likely feel either shame or a short-term motivation to diet and exercise because of the new celebrity body everyone is holding up as the ideal. But it doesn't stop there. I'm sure body comparison sneaks into your life in everyday ways with

everyday people like it did with me.

Interestingly, the Bible doesn't spend time focusing instruction on maintaining a healthy body, and it certainly doesn't outline "how-to" tips for a perfect bikini body. But we do. I find that when we're obsessed with things God doesn't seem to care much about, we might be missing something. A chance to lean in to more of what God wants for us, and a chance to live in and with our bodies without continual angst. Wouldn't that be beautiful?

Writer Shauna Niequist says, "My body gives me the opportunity to demonstrate grace, to make peace with imperfection every time I see myself in the mirror."[8]

I love that. The idea that we can give grace, speak grace, and live with grace when it comes to our bodies. Whether it's when you're alone in a bathtub under the stars, or sitting on the edge of a public pool surrounded by people, or in a gym with your friends.

I'll be honest here. While I think

Dig up a baby picture and put it on the fridge or in a frame. It's a way of giving grace to your grown-up body. It's an exercise of grace over imperfection. Because your baby self and your grown-up self are the same person. So let's love them both.

I've gotten close and cozy with demonstrating grace when it's just my body and me; I still struggle with the bathing suit body in a public space. But since I am inching toward wellness, wholeness, or whatever you'd like to call being comfortable on the beach in a bathing suit, I'll let you in on two of the secrets that have helped me.

One, love your baby self.

I truly came to terms with my body when I was thirty-three years old. My youngest child, Sara, was three years old. She was standing naked in front of the tub waiting for me as I prepped for her bath. I grabbed a towel and baby shampoo, then I turned to see her tiny body, all round and soft, pressed up against the tub as she splashed the water pouring out of the spout. I smiled and sighed. I wanted to scoop her little cherub body into my arms and squeeze her. The mother love was so intense and proud. And then I had the most startling revelation. I realized she looked just like me.

I've seen baby pictures of myself in the pool and in the tub at three years old. And that child standing in front of me was a direct duplication. Her tummy was soft, her rear end round and feminine. Tiny hands and feet. A headful of curly blonde hair. I stared at her, thinking about how much I adored her little body, but not so much my own.

I was a demanding drill sergeant with my own body, a tender mother toward my daughter's. It was a changing point for me. I wanted to love my body like I loved hers. With that picture in my head, I worked toward lavishing as much mental acceptance and love on myself as I did toward my daughter.

Sometime later, I found a picture I had snapped of Sara playing in the tub, and I hunted down a photo of myself playing in the tub at the same age. Then I put both of them on the fridge as a continual reminder for me to love my self.

I've shared this story with a lot of

dear daughters. And I've told them all the same thing: love your baby self. Dig up a baby picture and put it on the fridge or in a frame. It's a way of giving grace to your grown-up body. It's an exercise of grace over imperfection. Because your baby self and your grown-up self are the same person. So let's love them both.

Two, look at the whole picture.

We tend to be incredibly myopic about our bodies. We see only what's standing right in front of us, on the other side of the mirror. And while remembering your baby self is important to understanding how to love your body, it's also really helpful to think about and visualize your body growing old. I know, it's counterintuitive. Because culture teaches us to brace against the aging body. But there is something lovely and restful about accepting and appreciating the fact that you're growing older.

If we were more holistic about our bodies, we'd be much more inclined to see further out and to practice more gratitude. Try this. Think on your body as a tiny baby self, then wander along in your imagination and see your body at seven years old. And eleven years old. And now, eighteen. Now walk on into your early twenties. And so on, until you reach today, all the while practicing acceptance at every age.

Now. The riskier part. Wander five years from where you are now and think of what your body might look like then. I know you haven't reached it yet, but try to go there. And then add on another ten years successively, until you reach seventy years old. What do you see?

I see my hair piled in a loose bun on top of my head. I'm at the barn, in breeches and a soft white t-shirt. I'm sporting a little tan, and, of course, my face is much more wrinkled. But here's what I'm doing: I'm teaching my granddaughter how to ride. Yes, I'm older. Yes, my body has seen a lot of change. But my body and I are doing what we love with whom we love.

After that exercise, do you know what happens when I look at my imperfect but lovely fifty-four-year-old body? I feel young, fit, fabulous. I love my body. I appreciate my body. Because I see the whole picture. And I see what bodies are good for: for getting us where we want to be and helping us do what we want to do. For letting us exist in the same spaces as the people we love.

As your midcentury spiritual mama, I can promise you this: No matter what kind of awesome shape you're in, when you hit thirty or forty or fifty years old, you're going to have some things that bother you that you can't fix. Nora Ephron wrote, "Anything you think is wrong with your body at the age of thirty-five you will be nostalgic for at the age of forty-five."[9] It's so true. At thirty-five, I cursed my butt in jeans. Thought it was crazy-awful that I was wearing jeans two sizes larger than in my twenties. What a joke. I'd pay big money to have that butt back now.

Instead of indulging the nostalgic hunger by trying to reach back and regain what's been lost forever, or trying to create something modeled after a picture in a magazine or your friend lying out at the pool next to you, try taking a deep collective breath and thank God for the body you have. I mean, is your complexion really that bad? Are you maybe just a touch too hard on yourself when your face breaks out? Have you stopped wearing shorts because you think your thighs are too big?

We have a saying around this house. Anytime someone wonders out loud about things like this, we respond with, "While you're young and beautiful, baby." We ripped it off from Carrie Underwood's song, "We're Young and Beautiful," because she says, "The time will come when we're not so young and beautiful."[10] I mean, it's the truth, right? So while you're young and beautiful, get yourself in a swimsuit and wear those shorts.

But do you find there is there a big

mental roadblock for you? Do you look at your body critically, holding a little scorecard like a judge in the Miss America Pageant? Is it flat-out hard for you to thank God for your body? Then I'd love for you to get curious. Why are you hating the one body that you got? Where did it start for you? And what do you want to do about it?

If I could, I'd have you come to my gentle yoga class. We'd unroll our mats side by side. And then Shanin', my instructor, would lead us through a class alongside other women I've gotten to know.

There's Amy; she's in her twenties. Then Nancy; she's about my age. And then there's Rhonda Kay. She's retired, so I think she's in her late sixties or early seventies. She's about five feet tall, and loves wearing colorful caftans she makes herself and lots of different bracelets stacked on her wrists.

I love knowing Rhonda Kay because she is an older woman who is good with her body. I can just tell. She wears form-fitting clothes at yoga.

While many of the older women
drape t-shirts over their bodies in
class, Rhonda Kay doesn't. I aspire to
this kind of lack of self-consciousness.
Beyond that, this is a woman who is a
breast cancer survivor who appreciates
her one beautiful life. She takes her
grandkids to the water park. She is
the unpaid, unofficial greeter at the
yoga studio. Always checking in with
everyone, asking how they're feeling.
She is all grace and peace with herself.
And the most beautiful part is that's
what she exudes to me and everyone
she meets.

I think, until you are able to extend
grace toward yourself, it's going to be
awfully hard to extend grace toward
other people. Grace flows from the
inside out.

What kind of guts would it take
to stand in front of a mirror naked
and say out loud, "Thank you, God,
for the gift of my body"? I highly
recommend it. Because your soul can't
settle in peaceful with a body you hate.
And the God truth is this: the whole

earth is filled with his glory. And that includes you.

You are God's glory. He created you. He loves you. Wouldn't it be lovely if you loved yourself too?

dear daughters

Susie Davis

Chapter Four:

On Your Relationship with Your Father

Chapter Four:

On Your Relationship with Your Father

This is and has been the Father's work from the beginning – to bring us into the home of his heart.

— George Macdonald

As I write this, Father's Day is just around the corner. I look forward to celebrating my 85-year-old father. He is a good man. And he loves me. I know this because he tells me he loves me, and he tells me he's proud of me and my family every chance he gets.

He is a spiritual man. Loves God and shares his faith with anyone who will listen. He is a provider and protector. Extremely demonstrative in his faith and love of family. I feel very fortunate to have him in my life. Humbled, really, that this is how things worked out for me. I have come to realize, sadly, that my situation is rare.

Every day I meet women who

have had negative relationships with their dads. Whether that means they had an absent dad, or an abusive one, or a dad who didn't take loving care of his family. And it's truly a heartbreak because the father-daughter relationship not only impacts the mental and emotional health of a woman but also her spiritual health.

Recently a dear daughter who just finished her sophomore year in college shared her "dad" story with me. They had a great family. Her parents were married over two decades. A picture-perfect life with all the things people dream of having. Good schooling, plenty of money, loving Christian home. And then boom. This dear daughter's world falls apart upon discovery of her father's unfaithfulness to her mother.

In the days that followed, story upon story unfolded revealing this man's dual life. And here is this girl in the middle of it all, struggling to understand who her dad really is, why he did what he did, and how that impacts her current and future life.

After going to counseling to deal with the fallout, her counselor suggested she write her dad a letter. She shared the letter with me and gave me permission to share it. I want to read a little bit of it to you. It's extremely honest and vulnerable.

She wrote:

Dad. When you tell me you'll never leave me or have never left me, I feel wildly conflicted and confused. Your actions took away my innocence, my fun-loving self, and left a burden, and along with it, this example that love expires and people are disposable.

This letter brought me to tears. For the girl who wrote it and for the father who received it, because there is a chasm in their relationship that will take years to repair.

Whether you've had a dad like this dear daughter, or a dad like mine, there is a fundamentally important issue to consider. Your dad is or was likely one of the most influential persons in your life, whether you like it or not. For some of us, it's easier to avoid thinking about our dads, or to pretend we don't need them. Even if our dads were wonderful, it can be uncomfortable to think about how they've shaped our lives, both positively and negatively. But they matter to the people we are today.

I remember sitting on the couch with my dad and mom when I was a freshman in college and telling them that I finally picked a major: Child Development. My dad sat thoughtful for a moment and then said, "Do you need a college degree for something like that?"

His comment was honest and not at all demeaning. His question was not meant to dissuade me from pursuing Child Development, but it did. I went back to Baylor, and over the next year and a half, I changed my major to Education, then to Communication, then Fashion Design, then back to Communication. I finally ended up majoring in General Studies which actually suited me just fine because I got to take all kinds of classes I was really interested in. It fit my Enneagram seven (defined as the "enthusiast") self just perfectly.

I tell you this because my dad didn't realize that as he sat across from me and asked a simple question, it could send me off in search of a major that would make him proud. Or please him. But it did. That's how influential he was in my life.

What about you? How has your dad influenced you? It's important to consider because there is a very strong chance you view your relationship with God through the lens of your relationship with your dad. Let me say that again. It is highly likely that you see your heavenly Father through the relationship of your earthly father.

Let that soak in a minute.

So, if that is true, you have to do the work to figure out you and your dad and your relationship

What about you? How has your dad's personality influenced how you think of your heavenly Father's personality? I think if you're honest, you'll start to see how sometimes you lump your heavenly Father and your dad together.

with him. How would you describe your relationship? And how have your dad's personality, family values, and spirituality impacted how you view God's character?

It's a big thing to think about.

The reason I'm tackling this with you is because it's the number one thing my dear daughters, the ones I'm personally mentoring, have had to understand in order to stand up free and whole in their relationship with God. It's also the thing that they have to unpack in order to see where they're going in life and why they react to things the way they do.

This concept that you look at God through the lens of your relationship with your dad has huge implications. I say that with confidence—whether you feel that you've had a great relationship with your dad or a not-so-great one.

It's natural for us to try to define the hugeness of God, and since God is called Father throughout Scripture (as a matter of fact, that was Jesus' favorite name for God), we're inclined to see God through our earthly fathers.

But there's a problem with that, because your dad and mine are just humans like us. Our dads stumble through life learning things; they make mistakes; they have sinned against God and man. And it's not disrespectful to say that; it's just the truth of who we all are as people. We've all sinned and fallen short.

But then, of course, God is God. He has never made mistakes; He has never sinned and never will. He is holy. Big distinction there.

But sometimes we erase the distinction. And things get blurry.

So, when I was little, I remember my dad could get tense and irritated over life things: a volatile day for the stock market, for instance, which is pretty understandable, considering he was a stockbroker at the time. He wasn't usually irritated with me, but I was a sensitive kid. So I noticed. I took it in.

When I met Jesus at twelve, it was

all rainbows and butterflies. I loved
reading about Jesus, how he told
stories to fishermen and hugged kids.
But when I thought about God the
Father, I figured he was like my dad.
That sometimes he got upset about
things.

So, when I did something wrong,
I thought that God was probably
irritated by that. And sometimes when
I asked forgiveness, I still felt there
was a lingering something between
the Father and me. I tended to see
God the Father through the lens of my
human dad.

What about you? How has your
dad's personality influenced how
you think of your heavenly Father's
personality? I think if you're honest,
you'll start to see how sometimes you
lump your heavenly Father and your
dad together.

One dear daughter that I mentor
has come to realize this. Her dad
abandoned her family when she
was little. Then her mom ended up
remarrying several times. Throughout

her young life, this dear daughter made poor decisions—in school, with guys, and with friends until, finally, her mom committed her to a school that took in troubled kids.

She struggled greatly in understanding that God was close and personal, taking great interest in all the details of her life. And that's easy to understand, yes? What with her father ignoring her and then the string of stepdads that came along afterward, each of them an imperfect stand-in for her heavenly Father.

For me, I not only thought of God in terms of my own father's imperfections; I also saw my heavenly Father as creative, demonstrative, and fun. I saw him as a provider and a safe place, which were also the ways that I saw my dad. See how that works?

Right or wrong, good or bad, your dad has had a lot of influence in your idea of God. And when you think a certain way about God, it causes you to react to him in a certain way. The dear daughter I mentioned found herself running into unhealthy relationships in order to feel the love she felt she lacked.

How about you? In what ways have you acted as if God has the personality or tendencies of your dad?

Hopefully and prayerfully, you're starting to see and understand how maybe you've missed God because of some shortsightedness regarding your dad. And in this, I don't mean to criticize your dad any more than I would criticize mine. It's just that seeing God rightly is important in your relationship with him. Because you are his daughter. Deeply loved, highly valued, and completely acceptable just as you are. So more than anything, I hope you'll see God with right eyes. Because it's then you see his love for you. And his love for your dad. And it's then that you start to sort out how to love God with all your energy, all your life, and love your neighbor (that, of course, includes your dad) as yourself.

That's my paraphrase of the greatest commandment via Jesus. Kind of my life goal, and my goal for my people. To love God with all your energy, all your life. I want that for all of us. I've spent my life trying to communicate that to all kinds of people in all kinds of situations. And that includes you.

Because I want you to know that you have a Father who knows you and loves you and would spend anything and everything to be in relationship with you. He really is the greatest dad.

He is called the Father of all comfort.[11] The God who strengthens the weary.[12] He knows everything about you and loves you.[13]

If you really deeply knew that God was the world's greatest dad, how would you respond to him differently?

Susie Davis

. . . .

. . . .

. . . .

. . . .

. . . .

. . . .

. . . .

. . . .

. . . .

. . . .

. . . .

. . . .

. . . .

dear daughters

Susie Davis

Chapter Five:

On Expectations

Chapter Five:

On Expectations

*Honesty and transparency make you
vulnerable. Be honest and transparent
anyway.*

— Mother Teresa

Clouds lay thin and gray against
the Texas sky, straining to
keep the sun from scorching
my yard. The zinnias in my garden
stand steady but fragile, their leaves
browning from braving endless days of
ninety-degree weather.

I walk outside to relieve my garden,
spraying water here and there. A
wasp nesting under the eaves swings
down into the mist zipping back and
forth like a child running through
a sprinkler on a hot day. I glance
around, realizing the grass is badly
parched. The heat is winning. I coil up
the hose and walk inside.

This sweltering day in Austin is
just one little day in a string of what

seem like endless summer days. It doesn't feel particularly special. I am not expecting anything spectacular to happen. Honestly, I am only hoping to stay cool for one hot minute, but even that is met with some internal skepticism.

For certain, this is not the kind of day that reminds you of Christmas. Not the day you envision joyous homecomings, cozy fires, and a Fraser fir wrapped in sentimental ornaments. Or a big sit-down dinner, followed by fabulous homemade pie and a viewing of *It's a Wonderful Life*. Not that BIG day that we overload with all kinds of BIG expectations, like we do at Christmas. And yet this low-expectation kind of summer day was exactly the kind where I found myself stressing about Christmases years ago.

Being in ministry has always necessitated financial creativity. So for a solid ten years of my marriage, I thought about Christmas gift-giving nearly all year long. I remember our early Christmases as a married couple.

I was intimidated by great gift-givers with big budgets. I felt small, always under-gifting in return.

After a couple Christmases of feeling deflated, I thought I found a way to wiggle around the inevitable diminishment: I started shopping sales all year in an attempt to buy things I thought family and friends would like when Christmastime came around.

It was kind of an obsession, the determination to keep up by getting ahead. Like working a puzzle, trying to find creative or trendy things for brothers, sisters, nieces, and nephews months in advance, using money saved by couponing at the grocery store week after week.

I'd finally find something, a name-brand shirt or designer whatchamadoo, just anything that I thought said, "I really care about you. See how I care about you." Then I'd record the purchase on my Christmas list and tuck it away in the depths of my closet, like a squirrel hoarding and stockpiling.

In early November, I'd pull out my
treasures, lay them out across the floor
and group them together by family.
They never seemed as fabulous then,
all those months later. In fact, there
were times I was sure the purchase was
a complete fail. There I was, staring
at that clearance Ralph Lauren coin
purse, knowing exactly why it was
on clearance in the first place. It just
wasn't cute. It wasn't necessary. It was
a pointless knickknack that nobody
needed. And now I was stuck.

It was miserable feeling that our
budget mandated my affection. And
I hated how gift-giving seemed to
stymie our identity as a couple. But
that's exactly how I felt: that somehow
this ministry salary left me
helplessly under-resourced.
I know it sounds kind of
pitiful on the page. I mean, my
gracious, we had a house to
live in and food in our stomachs
In light of the big wide world, we
were ridiculously over-privileged.
I'm just talking about it here because

it's an expectation we often have, and I don't want you to stress out or feel shame if you can't buy a bunch of expensive gifts over a holiday season—or ever. It's not worth the hassle, loading up with a bunch of stuff that couldn't even begin to tell people how you really feel about them.

As a matter of fact, you know what? For all the Christmases that have come and gone, it's not the gifts that are remembered or even the "BIG DAY" itself. Because the "BIG DAYS" (Thanksgiving, Christmas, Easter, etc.) are usually cram-packed with a lot of travel, too much food, and excess anxiety. Maybe you've felt the same way.

It's weird and wrong to pile so many expectations on those sweet days. Think back on some of your most meaningful days with the people you love. What was it that made the day special? I bet it wasn't a gift at all. Write that down and remember it when you feel the holiday pressure with all the expectations coming at you.

I want you to be free. Free to join the traditions, free to break from traditions. Just free to spend your time and money and energy doing what it is God leads you to in your one beautiful life.

In an attempt to relieve those special holidays from all the craziness here's a kind of monumental idea: no leaning on gifts to express affection, and no ridiculous spending.

No fretful catalogue-stalking late into the night, wondering how to get it all done on whatever budget we have. And no Pinteresting impossible, expensive crafts to make with our little uncrafty hands. Christmas is not meant to be that kind of BIG DEAL.

And just as you shouldn't place undue exceptions on yourself, let's agree not to place them on each other either. I mean, wouldn't the world be a lovelier place if we could all promise not to make getting together on the BIG DAYS such a BIG DEAL that hurt feelings sneak into our relationships about trips missed or plans changed on those days? Just think how free we'd feel if we stopped being dramatic about making one or two days a year BIG DAYS when there are so many in between to enjoy.

Here's how I want to be with my

very own family. If my children happen to be spending holidays with their in-laws or even if work keeps them away or even if it's their very own grown-up decision to stay at their very own house for Christmas, I will not fret or freak out. Of course we want to see them, but it doesn't have to be at Christmas or Thanksgiving or the Fourth of July or any other holiday during the year. Because you know what? All the in-between days matter just as much as the BIG DAYS.

There are 365 days in a year to remember people in thoughtful, inexpensive, and even cost-free ways. A call, a text, a funny photo shared. An old-fashioned letter or a homemade loaf of bread. A hug, a smile, an unexpected visit. There are so many ways we can love one another, and so many days to choose from.

What if instead of defaulting to buying things for each other, we all thought about creative ways to shower affection, like time and words and actions that have nothing to do with holiday cheer or gifts under the tree? I know it's a complete turnaround on the holidays. But just think over it now. What are three or four ways you could show affection without buying things?

I guess what I mean for me and my house is this: I refuse to measure our relationship by gifts or holidays. I'm prayerful that's your heart, too.

And that brings me to another something. How about working on setting boundaries so that "tradition" doesn't become "expectation."

Here's how a tradition works: someone starts something. It's happy and fun and easy. It makes people feel connected and lovely. But over the years, in an effort to hang on to that connected and lovely feeling, it starts to feel like expectation. If you don't show up or participate, suddenly you're kind of anti-family. You're dissing the people you love.

The thing to remember is that it's okay to outgrow a family tradition. And that doesn't mean you're

outgrowing your family. When we get hung up on the thing we do instead of the people we do it with, it's wacky and our love is upside-down.

So the big question is this: How do you get out of a tradition-slash-expectation and still honor people in the process? I think we all have to be big boys and girls. Which is actually very difficult. Because not everyone is willing to part with traditions. And not everyone is able to see how traditions can take a nasty turn toward expectations. It's then you might feel caught, folding into the tradition just to make peace at your own expense. Which is people-pleasing. Which is fear. Which is for another conversation, a whole other chapter, and possibly some therapy.

So dear daughters, here is the deal: I want you to be free. Free to join the traditions, free to break from traditions. Just free to spend your time and money and energy doing what it is God leads you to in your one beautiful life. So please consider every tradition as an invitation that you may accept or decline.

Just be gentle in your communication, especially in instances where there is a "no" to a tradition that's been in full swing for, say, twenty years or so. Think ahead of time. Respond as early as necessary. If it's a twenty-year tradition, a year's notice might be necessary.

Your first priority will always and ever be your husband, your children—even just yourself, as an adult with her own life, her own community, her own responsibilities. I talk to my kids honestly and explain that I do not assume that the traditions we had as a family will always fit into their best interest as a family. If they do, I will shout and clap and celebrate. If they don't, I commit to look for a way to respect their decision without hurt feelings, even if it takes therapy. And I'm not joking. I would gladly go to therapy to learn how to be a big girl and deal with any disappointment they might unintentionally deal me.

Speaking of disappointment, we're going to all have our fair share. Because it's life. Life is full of disappointment, even with people you love to the moon and back. My family will disappoint me; I'll disappoint them. The dysfunction sets in when we're too scared to talk about all the things. Then we're walking on eggshells. Trying to keep fake peace with each other. Which is no peace at all. Instead it's talking behind closed doors and whispering and working hard to hold together a big broken mess of a family.

I won't have it in my family. Because I love them too much to let our relationships be fake and uneasy. So I'm committed to talk about the hard things and cry over them and then hug it out. I want to be the best kind of person in their life. The very best.

I'm not saying it will be perfectly easy, but I promise you this: I am not going to be a seventy-year-old mother who expects her daughter to coerce an entire family to "grandma's house"

for Christmas morning three states
away. No siree. Not me. And I'm
not going to require a big breakfast
with milk punch and affirmations on
Christmas morning (a Davis family
tradition) if it isn't something my kids
feel comfortable with. By all means,
I want them to tell me. Because
I'm 100 percent more interested in
supporting who they are and spending
time with them than I am in holding
on to something. Traditions should
strengthen a family, not diminish it.

Honestly think over your traditions
with your family. Are they still
contributing to the health of your
family? If not, is there a gentle way to
talk about it with the people you love?
Write down the things you love about
the holidays and the things that drain
you. Then be willing to talk about it.
It can be difficult, but in the long run,
there are so many benefits when you
are honest in your relationships.

I guess in the end, I just want to
encourage kindness to all. And yet
to be firm about our own needs and

feelings as we know them on the days we come together. Christmas will always be a conundrum. I'm not sure Jesus would like his birthday celebration cluttered and confused by things that in the end don't matter much at all.

Let's uncomplicate things with excessive kindness as we each seek to love God and each other well. Let's celebrate the best gift he's giving us: each other.

Susie Davis

dear daughters

Susie Davis

Chapter Six:

On Feeling Small

Chapter Six:
On Feeling Small

I seek little opportunities, mere trifles, to give pleasure to Jesus; for instance, a smile, a pleasant word when inclined to be silent and to show weariness.

— St. Thérèse of Lisieux

My week started off a lot like yours, I bet. Just checking things off the list. And by that, I mean doing the everyday things that don't even get written down. The boring things: doing laundry, cleaning out the fridge, emptying the dishwasher.

I felt grumpy because I thought if I could only finish these unimportant things, I could get to the good stuff. The meaningful stuff, like writing something or recording a podcast episode or returning an important email.

Instead, there I stood in my pajamas, folding laundry on top of the little white enamel table in my washroom.

Through the window, I saw a tiny hummingbird sipping on the purple salvia. I sighed out loud and went back to folding towels, feeling small and humdrum and, honestly, kind of sorry for myself. If only I had more time or more help, then I could get to the good things.

And then I remembered the words I've been reading, written by Brother Lawrence, in *Practicing the Presence of God*. I found this treasure of a book at an estate sale. It has a pink and gold cover—super retro. I just love it. It's a deep read, but short. I highly recommend it. Here's what he says:

> *We can do little things for God; I turn the cake that is frying on the pan for love of Him, and that done, if there is nothing else to call me, I prostrate myself in worship before Him, Who has given me grace to work; afterwards I rise happier than a king. It is enough for me to pick up but a straw from the ground for the love of God.*[14]

Ahhh, it's so convicting. Because his "turning of the cake" is my folding laundry. Small menial tasks that someone has to do. But while I was wishing myself out of them, he was worshipping in them.

You, too, must have a long list of things to do that seem unimportant. Things that seem to get in the way of doing what actually matters. What are those things for you? The small, humdrum tasks that seem to steal the time and energy you'd like to spend elsewhere? Make a mental list. Or even write a few down on paper.

Here's my list today: make the bed, water the plants, feed the cat. Go to the grocery store, write a thank you note, call Mom and Dad. These are not the things that make news, that's for sure. And I struggle to think that my list even causes God to take notice, like I'm awash in a world of things that are insignificant. I'm not off giving humanitarian aid to people in need or endangering my life to share the Gospel, after all.

So the loveliest news: Brother Lawrence says doing small things doesn't inhibit doing something really big for God. And that's worshipping him. Flip the cake, worship God. Fold the laundry, thank him for the "grace to work."

So yeah, folding laundry in my PJs and talking with God is big stuff in kingdom currency. And no matter where you are in your day, that is important to God too. Whether you're changing diapers or driving to work or unloading dishes, if we keep our hearts open to God in the midst of the mundane, that matters to him.

We've just got life all mixed up though, don't we? Thinking we need to finish XYZ in order to do something significant, while in reality, we are right now in the thick of it with God. That's really valuable to him.

Oswald Chambers also talked of life and the little things. He wrote:

Beware of allowing yourself to think that the shallow aspects of life

*are not ordained by God; they are
ordained by Him equally as much as
the profound. The shallow amenities
of life, eating and drinking, walking
and talking, are all ordained by God.
These are the things in which our
Lord lived.*[15]

The things in which Jesus lived.
Doing laundry? Yes, probably so.
Making dinner? You bet. He tended
things the same as you and me. He
lived in the shallow and the deep. He
was a human, and that's what being
human is: big things and little things
in equal measure. And this is how
God ordained it. So how do we get to
thinking on things the way God does?

First, we stop looking so much at
what other people are doing. I don't
think I'm overblowing this by
saying that we know more about
our neighbors and their day-to-
day lives than at any time in history.
Social media has changed the way we
look at the world. It's ridiculously easy
to get online and explore the "big"

It is dangerous to judge your value by what other people are doing—it's then that you diminish your own life. You believe that somehow, someway, your life isn't inherently valuable just as it is.

Susie Davis

things people are doing and to then
feel even smaller by comparison. Easy
to look through a tiny phone screen
thinking everyone else is off living
adventurously or serving God in
visible ways.

It is dangerous to judge your value
by what other people are doing—it's
then that you diminish your own life.
You believe that somehow, someway,
your life isn't inherently valuable
just as it is. And isn't that the most
depressing thought? That we're sucked
into a mindset where our lives are, at
their very core, unimportant?

It's like this: Much of my time is
spent doing the menial thing. So if my
view is that God doesn't give a care
about teeny, tiny me down in Austin,
Texas, standing in my PJs folding
laundry, then I have a worthless life.
And if I believe I have a worthless life,
I either become despondent or strive
to make my life worthwhile by doing
certain things or trying to become a
certain someone. We choose to either
embrace the fact that God cares about

even the small things we do, or we reject it.

So what will you do? Accept your life as lovely and valuable to God right where you are, doing what you're doing? Or step outside of that God reality and try to make yourself more important?

I know it's anti-cultural to adopt a "small is important" kind of life. But think on this: What if Jesus had rejected all the "small" things in his life and strived for more? I doubt very much that we would have a Savior. I don't think he would have chosen to do the things he did. Instead he stayed wholly focused on God's plans for his life, which included becoming so small that he died a criminal's death.

The thought of it crushes me into gratitude because it means doing small things doesn't make me small, either. Even being mistreated doesn't make me small. It's actually in dying to striving for importance that makes me big. When I choose serenity inside the

small places in my life, I am following in his footsteps.

So yes, that means I get over the mental battle with my ego (because it is my ego trying to mark "small" as "unimportant") and start thanking God for my assignments right where I am.

Which brings me to my second thought: gratitude is paramount to inner significance. And gratitude starts right where you are, in your everyday life.

So for me, it means saying, "Thank you, God, for nice warm towels to fold. Thank you for this cute little enamel table I found secondhand. For the way folding laundry calms me and slows me down. Thank you for this chance to have a quiet minute with you. Thank you."

What about you? Look at your to-do list as an opportunity for creative worship. Where is the hidden worship in your list of things to do?

One more quote from Brother Lawrence. He says, "We must make our hearts a spiritual temple, wherein to adore him incessantly." How do we get to ceaseless worship? Sweep out the thinking that in life there is a big line dividing important work and unimportant work. Sit squarely inside this idea of "grace to work" and gratitude, relentlessly adoring God.

Does that sound outlandish? Unattainable? Ask God for help. What does your prayer sound like? Speak it out, write it out, get it out. And realize, even in the asking, that you are entering into the act of adoring God as your provider.

I'll leave you with Thérèse de Lisieux's words. She says, "Holiness consists simply in doing God's will, and being just what God wants us to be."

Here is what God wants me to be today: a garden-tender, an errand-runner, a house-tidier, a note-writer, a wife, a daughter.

I am reminded that when I am doing those simple, little things, I am pleasing him.

I hope this was a reminder to you too.

Susie Davis

dear daughters

Susie Davis

Chapter Seven:

On Transitions

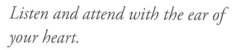

Chapter Seven:

On Transitions

Listen and attend with the ear of your heart.

– Saint Benedict

After my ride at the barn on Thursday, I found myself at Shoal Creek Nursery. And there before my eyes were gorgeous, bright, beautiful zinnias. Pink, yellow, orange. Just tons of them, begging me to take them with me. Before I knew it, I had filled the back of my car to overflowing. Yep, all those zinnias were coming home with me.

So on top of my regular schedule of work and home chores, I impulsively added in swapping out the spring flowers for summer flowers in all three garden beds. Which ended up being a really big job. It took me all day to finish that up.

The very next evening, I added

another something to my regular
week. I invited my big extended family
for dinner Friday night. All thirty-six
of them. I did lots of little extra things
to try and make it special. Good stuff,
fun stuff. My mind kept reminding me
of all the things that needed attention.
My body complied. I did it all.

But after my family left that evening
and after staying up way too late
cleaning up, my feet started hurting.
Between my ride, the flowers and the
party, I knew I had pushed too hard.
When I finally got to bed, I had the
hardest time falling asleep because I
had triggered a pain syndrome I have
that creates a weird ache all over my
body but especially in my hands and
feet. My body was reminding my
mind that it had overdone it with my
extra-long to-do list. My mind kept
pushing and pushing with all the fun
ideas and all the extras—good things,
fun things—but honestly, too many
things.

The next morning, while my body
was recouping, I sat and thought

about you. Do you let your mind boss your body around too? Take a second and think on the ways you are pushing yourself and why. I'm asking you this because we're going somewhere with it. Because I figure you are a lot like me and sometimes you end up exhausted, but you don't know why. You get to bed late, wake up early, and all you have is a lot of tiredness with little understanding to how you got there. Or at least little understanding on the why behind all the striving and hustling.

It could be that, like me, you hurt because you pushed and ignored the signals your body was sending. That's one way the hustle browbeats us. Or it could be that your mind pushed you into thinking your to-do list was more important than taking care of your body. Like skipping workouts, yoga, or things like that.

So really, take a minute and think on this: How does your mind boss your body around?

I'm betting there are ways your

mind keeps you running. Maybe
it's a to-do list at work or maybe it's
your overflowing closet that needs
attention. Could be those little ones.
Kids certainly have a way of kicking
things into overdrive. But something,
whether big or small, keeps you
looking to the next thing. Sometimes
you probably go weeks, or maybe
even months, getting pushed around
by your overbearing mind, but you
don't think too much about it because
you're in a rhythm of physical rest
nightly. But the exhaustion is there,
weighing on you, whether you realize
it or not.

After my Friday family
gathering, the very next
evening, a Saturday, Will
and I taught at church
together. It was great but
also very tiring, and when I
fell asleep that night, I felt a tiny
bit sad. Not sure why.

Then Sunday morning, I woke up,
had coffee, and sat to journal and
read but instead, I just cried. It wasn't

a big ugly cry but a steady stream of
tears. The kind that make you feel like
crawling right back into bed. I wasn't
sure exactly why I was crying. I knew
it was a mix of things. Some of it likely
had to do with being physically tired.

But some of it had to do with being
emotionally tired. Tired out from
the usual stuff that comes from the
sometimes-complicated dynamics of
being a pastor's wife, and also a little
tiny piece of sadness from just missing
my kids on Mother's Day weekend,
which happened to be that weekend.
They're all grown up and happy, and
I'm so glad about that. But I also really
miss them. An achy, deep kind of
missing only a mama can know.

So I sat and cried, coffee in hand,
and Will walked in. He offered to let
me stay home, not teach the other two
services. I pondered it. Cried a little
more. Sat still and quiet. Then I let my
heart speak.

I told Will about why church often
felt so heavy and hard and lonely for
me. I spoke about missing the kids but

Wholehearted living comes as we acknowledge the incongruencies going on between our feelings and our thoughts. Between what we're willing ourselves to do despite the quiet nudges deep in our soul telling us otherwise.

being happy they're grown and gone, living their one beautiful life with their people. The mix of that dichotomy. I talked about the sadness of having a chronic pain syndrome and not being able to physically do all the things I'd love to do. I spoke up about the sadness over a relationship that soured, how I felt a person was being passive-aggressive toward me, and how it drained me.

I cried, sipped coffee, and cried. It was messy and inconvenient. It was bad timing to have all the feelings on a morning when I was teaching. But here is the thing: I gave my heart voice. I let it speak. And that is important. And something I'd like to talk about with you. Are you letting your heart have voice in your life? Or better yet, are you living your one beautiful life with your whole heart?

Wholehearted living comes as we acknowledge the incongruencies going on between our feelings and our thoughts. Between what we're willing ourselves to do despite the quiet nudges deep in our soul telling us otherwise.

Or are you pushing relentlessly, following your to-do list but all the while feeling a nagging sense that you're off course? Are you projecting what you think you should be or should look like as a Christian woman but feeling a little bit like a fraud? I am wondering: Do you have expectations of yourself that even God doesn't have for you?

Over the last two months, I've had two dear daughters and one spiritual mama come to me with these kinds of things. They were feeling stuck, worried, and anxious about their lives. Then after asking a few questions, talking things out, and walking metaphorically around their lives, we could all see clearly how, with their heads so focused on their issues, they weren't giving their hearts voice. They were having internal battles between their minds and hearts, and their minds were winning.

As they worked on their lives,

checking off things on the spiritual list, they were quieting the little cries of their hearts. And I do it too. By prioritizing, analyzing, thinking, planning, and working without giving any space to listening and feeling.

In the same way, I let my mind boss my body around; sometimes I let my mind shush my heart. Because listening and feeling can seem so unproductive. And it sounds so emotional to listen to what your heart is saying. The kind of thing you did as a teenager that grown-up you doesn't have time for. All the big feelings and the crazy, unorganized stuff that follows.

But here's where God is on that: Jesus says to love the Lord your God with all your heart, and with all your soul, and with all your mind and with all your strength.[16]

I think many of us just want to love God with our soul (personality), our mind (intellect) and might (ability) while dismissing the heart. But God asks for a holistic love, a wholehearted love. He also wants us to give life and voice to our hearts. Because that's how we are able to give and receive authentic affection, and that's when we truly love.

What about you? Can you relate? Will you be quiet for just a minute and try listening to your heart? What is your heart trying to tell you? And why? Think about the apparent incongruencies in your life that leave you feeling stymied or locked in. Why are they there?

Finally, I want you to consider why is your heart saying those things? If you are sad, why? If you are lonely, what's at the root? If you feel anxious, what is that springing from? Why is your heart saying those things?

I think when you start unpacking the why beneath what your heart is trying to speak, you'll be in a much more honest place with God. That's when you'll live a whole and authentic life before him.

Let me just reassure you right now, it's okay for you to feel those things. God made you with a big heart to feel all the feelings. And just because you're feeling them doesn't mean you will act on them. And it doesn't mean they rule you.

But I can give you a warning and tell you that if you live only in your head and ignore your heart, you're likely to end up really unhealthy.

In *Waking the Dead* (which is one of my tiptop favorites and I strongly recommend you read it), John Eldredge writes, "To remain present to God, you must remain present to your heart. To hear his voice, you must listen with your heart. To love him, you must love with all your heart. You cannot be the person God meant you to be, and you cannot live the life he meant you to live, unless you live from the heart."[17]

You must stop spending so much time in your head and be more aware of your heart. As a matter of fact, the Bible says you should guard your heart because it determines the course of your life.[18] Kinda hard to guard your tiny, tender little heart if you're ignoring her. Right?

You'll be glad to know that I had a good Sunday morning cry, and then I got dressed and went to church, where I taught both Sunday messages with Will. God blessed it. And good came out of it. But I also know this with all certainty: If I needed to stay home Sunday morning because my heart was too busted up, God would still love me just as much. And his work would be accomplished with or without me being there Sunday morning.

The same is true in your life too. God doesn't expect you to keep pushing and pushing and ignoring the call to wholehearted living. He doesn't think of you as a soldier; he thinks of you as a dearly loved daughter. And I do too.

There's one more quote from Eldredge I'll leave you with:

God loves you; you matter to him.

That is a fact, stated as a proposition.
I imagine most of you have heard
it any number of times. Why, then,
aren't we the happiest people on earth?
It hasn't reached our hearts.[19]

My prayer is that this truth reaches
you today right where you live and
settles deep inside your heart.

dear daughters

Susie Davis

. . . .

. . . .

. . . .

. . . .

. . . .

. . . .

. . . .

. . . .

. . . .

. . . .

. . . .

. . . .

Chapter Eight:

On Living Wholeheartedly

Chapter Eight:
On Living Wholeheartedly

We shake with joy, we shake with grief.
What a time they have, these two
housed as they are in the same body.
— Mary Oliver

When you come to my house, bright orange, pink, and yellow zinnias line the sidewalk cheering you on as you step up to the front French doors. Two large picture windows flank the doors with two black rocking chairs resting beside. And then, when you walk inside, you see right through the open living and dining space to a wall of windows framing the backyard, where the live oak drapes low, shading a swimming pool surrounded by vintage iron patio chairs. I found the chairs at an estate sale—they are all painted a lively Tiffany blue. Then just beyond is the Balcones Canyonland Preserve. It's one of the few green spaces in

Austin, and gratefully, it is protected from concrete encroachment. As you look up upon acres and acres of land, all that you see are the tips of trees reaching up to hug the big Texas sky.

But I'm laughing now, because you'll likely never get that grand green front door welcome. Everybody comes in our house through the side door by the garage and the air-conditioning unit. It's the closest entry if you park in the driveway, and everybody parks in our driveway. So in an effort to make the side entrance friendlier, I bought lots of pale pink geraniums and potted them in vintage art deco planters. I placed the pots alongside two small copper birdbaths under the enormous crepe myrtle tree by the side door. The tree's canopy is glorious, but it's so big you'd have to crank your head way back to see the mass of tiny white blossoms. All you really notice when you come to the side entrance is the giant trunk of the tree, which I think is pretty impressive. The bark is a dark, dappled-cinnamon color. Will says

that when the tree is losing its bark
in the summer time, it feels as soft
as a horse's muzzle. It's unusual and
gorgeous.

But if you don't know much about
crepe myrtles, the peeling bark might
look like the tree is not doing well. It
almost looks like a snake shedding its
skin. You might even think the tree
is sick. But it's not at all. It's just in a
season of transition.

Transitions, in nature and in our
own lives, are curiously beautiful.
Often messy, sometimes painful but
always miraculous in the end because
it means something new is being born.

Recently, I met with a dear daughter
over lunch at my favorite Austin
bistro. As lunch was ending, I asked
a question about how she was doing.
One question led to another, and then
she started talking with me about her
feelings regarding leaving a job she
loved and had worked at for over five
years. Not only was the job a joy to
her, but it also had deep roots in her
introduction to and early relationship

with God. But the season had come to an end. And with it, some important relationships changed in a significant and negative way.

I noticed tears spring to her eyes. I asked about the tears. We talked some more. And then she started really crying. The kind of cry that makes your cheeks turn red and makes it hard to catch your breath. No matter that we were sitting in a rather small, open, one-room restaurant where several tables full of people were finishing up lunch. The tears rolled steady down her face like rain on a window. She was grieving the change and the loss.

Transitions signal the death of one season as life brings forth another. And so, for most people, even if the new season is a good one, it's still hard. And it's especially hard if you don't like grieving. Or if you don't realize grief is sometimes necessary.

I would say I am still in a season of transition. In the last five years, all our children got married. And then they all moved away. That was one of the biggest and most difficult transitions I've been through because I loved mothering, and I love my people. My family is my heart, so having them leave and create new lives apart from me was hard. Healthy, yes. (Will always reminds me separation is the goal.) But oh so achy. So I have all the feelings: happy, sad, hopeful, anxious, and somewhere in the middle of it, just plain tired.

It was a chronic stream of these feelings that led me to find my mentor, Janet. I started meeting with her when I felt confused about my sadness. She has been pivotal in helping me understand that grief is a necessary part of transition. Janet reminds me that grief is a way of saying goodbye.

I know. Not what you or I want to hear. But it's truth. And the truth has a way of lining the path of sorrow with hope.

What about you? Are you in a season of transition, too? If you aren't,

Transitions require that we let loose of things. Sometimes that means we walk away from a job we loved or say goodbye to a relationship we enjoyed.... And then that we walk forward in our lives believing that God actually is with us and in us working his good pleasure.

you will be soon. Because transitions are a part of life. And transitions birth transformation. And that's what God is all about in your life and mine: transforming us more and more into his image through our everyday story. And isn't that the loveliest thought? That we don't have to go about scheduling in "growth" to our spiritual lives? He's right there, working it through the seasons in our lives.

Here's what I am learning: transitions require that we let loose of things. Sometimes that means we walk away from a job we loved or say goodbye to a relationship we enjoyed. It requires that we open our hands as well as our hearts. And then that we walk forward in our lives believing that God actually is with us and in us working his good pleasure. And hidden in his pleasure for our lives is our best good.

So for me, I open my hands and accept that a mothering role I love is now over, or at least really different. And as I open my hands, I signal to

my heart that it's okay to feel sad
that the most glorious thing I got
to do with my time and energy and
my body has passed. And I cry (I am
crying now), and then I count the
blessings I've had (could I ever begin
to list them?), and then because my
heart speaks truth, I acknowledge the
loss that the season I loved has ended.

While I'm all about good news,
positivity, and counting blessings, I
have discovered it's equally important
to list your losses. I can't tell you
how many times in the last year that
Janet has asked me to sit with the
discomfort and write down a list of
losses. It's hard to sit in grief when
you really just want to be
happy, but I have found
grieving makes way for a most
delicate, intimate joy with God.
So don't be afraid of grief. It
will pass if you unlock it and
let it fly away. It's only in listing losses
and allowing the hollow space that
you make room for the new things.

Do you have losses you need to

list? It's not hard if you let your heart speak. Say a prayer; ask God for help and sit in the quiet. Then think. What do you miss? What do you wish was still present that is now over? Here's a tiny piece of what my honest list of losses looks like: I miss my children. Not just who they are now, but who they were back then. Happy little voices, blocks scattered across the floor. Long, lazy mornings with breakfast of French toast and scrambled eggs. Intricate LEGO buildings and a Playmobile dollhouse sitting in the corner. I miss the mornings at the barn with my girls and their sandy, sun-kissed faces. I miss the little boy who would ask me to read him a book every night. The way each of my children would let me enfold them in a hug.

But now it is over. And I must "Give up all the other worlds except the one to which you belong."[20] I am learning to let go of certain "worlds" I have loved and treasured as I wait for the space where I belong. And I don't yet see the space where I belong. So yes, there are tears. Do you feel it too? Are you giving something up?

I learned something really insightful from my friend Alison Cook when she was on the Dear Daughters Podcast. She said in order to manage negative feelings, you must try and befriend them. Even the ones that you don't like. For me that would look like friending the sadness that comes with the end of my mothering job. The alternative would mean trying to shut down my sadness and lock it up. Or even worse, continuing to attempt to mother my young adult kids. And you know that woman, right? She turns into the mother-in-law no one wants to be around. Not at all what I'm aiming for.

No, I want to be a wise woman. A spiritual mama. I want to grow. But it feels messy. I feel messy. The kind of messy I don't want to be, the kind of messy I don't want anyone to see. And sometimes I wish people would just go through the front door, leaving me alone to go through this in private. But that's not what we're called to do. So I talk to Janet, and I'm talking to you now.

Yep, much like that crepe myrtle by my back door. Things are peeling back. I'm in a season of transition—not who I was, not yet who I want to be. I am waiting for a new season of growth. Wanting very much to have a canopy of gorgeous white blossoms with no peeling bark.

Do you know what I discovered about that crepe myrtle tree I wrote about earlier? There is a way to minimize or even eradicate the peeling of the bark, but only by lopping off the top of the tree. People who don't understand what's best for the tree do it to force a superficial design, but around here it's called "crepe murder." Not joking. (We love our trees down in Austin.) When they lop off the top, beheading the tree, it actually restricts its growth. Without the natural peeling process, the gorgeous canopy is stunted.

It just makes me wonder: How often do we attempt to force a superficial design in our lives at the expense of what naturally would be a gorgeous canopy?

What about you? What would it look like to befriend your emotions during this transition? Do you feel sad? Do you feel anxious? Do you feel overwhelmed? Lost? Instead of shaming yourself over those feelings, get curious about them and see what's at the root. And while we're talking about this, can I make one more suggestion? Talk to someone about them. Please. It would make this mother's heart so glad to think that you're not walking through this alone.

My heartfelt prayers for both of us are that we have vision for the beautiful things we don't yet see, that we settle in exactly where God has us, and that we celebrate in advance his good plans even if we are in a season of transition.

Susie Davis

dear daughters

Susie Davis

....

....

....

....

....

....

....

....

....

....

....

....

....

Chapter Nine:

On Finding Care For Your Soul

On Finding Care For Your Soul

I have more mothers than any eight girls off the street. They are the moons shining over me.

— Sue Monk Kidd

There is a time in every woman's life when she needs to find some comfort. A time when she needs an older, wiser woman walking just a few steps ahead who is ready to give a bit of wisdom and remind her that God is still in control, and that everything is going to be okay.

I certainly needed that in my life recently. It was a few months after the wedding of our youngest daughter, Sara. I was doing fine. I didn't have anything "tragical" going on (in the words of Anne Shirley, of Green Gables), but I still felt sort of off. Like I was meandering spiritually. My heart felt flat.

Around that time, I reached out
to Janet, a spiritual director here in
Austin whom I mentioned earlier. And
I have to tell you, after the very first
meeting, I felt so much better. Just
having someone listen to my story,
help me look for God in the details,
and respond with wisdom was life
changing.

When I stepped into that soul-care
relationship with Janet, I had a list of
things that I wanted to talk about. I
definitely wanted to sort through all
the feelings about three weddings in
five years—and why my kids getting
married was the happiest thing ever
but also brought a weird grief that,
quite honestly, I didn't feel like I
should talk about. But I also had
some foggy areas about my writing
life and whether I should continue
writing books. I wanted direction on
whether to venture into new ministry
opportunities. And I didn't exactly
know what to do about some relations
that had drifted over the years. When I
look at my list now, I see it was about

family, work, and friendship. So, kind
of big and important.

The thing I loved about meeting
with Janet is that our time and our
relationship was centered on me
hearing God in my life. That might
sound selfish because we don't talk a
lot about Janet's personal life. It's about
mine. But you know what, that's really
what I needed. So, I felt the cost was
well worth it—and yes, I really do pay
her. I like to think of our time as an
investment in me and my relationship
with God.

We're all about self-care for our
bodies (like doing yoga or playing
tennis), and we're about self-care for
our emotions (whether that's therapy
or hanging out with friends); but what
about self-care for our spirits?

So many dear daughters I know
go to Bible study or attend church
or even go to big Christian events,
and I think that is fantastic. But so
often, those things seem to be more
about studying and learning and not
listening. Who is helping you listen for

God's voice in your life? Who is taking the time to discern things with you about what God is saying in your life? Because having that kind of attention can give you perspective that helps you go from feeling overwhelmed to feeling really clear and compelled and connected to God.

Think about the people in your life who offer that kind of spiritual nurturing. I hope you have a friend or two like that. And maybe your husband if you're married. But I bet they also have another role in your life too. And I bet it sometimes blurs their ability to be the kind of keen advisers who helps you solely sort out God's quiet voice in your life.

How would your life be different if you could work with a mentor, spiritual director, or a spiritual mama? To have someone listen, then gently guide you to hearing God's voice? What kind of difference would it make for you?

In Sophie Hudson's book, *Giddy Up, Eunice* (which I highly recommend), she writes, "When the Holy Spirit in one woman recognizes and responds to the Holy Spirit in another woman, safe places become sacred spaces."[21]

I bet, like me, you need more sacred spaces in your life. Places where you stop, look around your life, and listen. And then crawl into the deep with God. I want that for you. Look around your world. Where are the sacred places? Whose face do you see?

When I look back over my life, I find sacred places everywhere, in the lives of everyday women who just happened to live close by. People who were truly formative to me in my spiritual life, my creative life, and my outlook on life. I can think of three women in particular.

Georgie Duwe lived just up the street from my family. Her daughter, Corbin, was my friend. Georgie's house was beautiful. When you walked in the front door, there was a big cage full of tiny colorful finches.

Who is taking the time to discern things with you about what God is saying in your life? Because having that kind of attention can give you perspective that helps you go from feeling overwhelmed to feeling really clear and compelled and connected to God.

There were floor-to-ceiling windows
off the living areas so you could see
the entire back yard, where Georgie
had large blooming potted plants.
They had a pool, a trampoline, a cozy
hidden courtyard leading to the master
bedroom. Under the bed in the master
bedroom, there was a tackle box of
costume jewelry. Georgie let us play
with her jewelry.

   As a matter of fact, Georgie let
Corbin and me do almost anything
we wanted: cook in the kitchen, have
camps in the backyard for the younger
kids in the neighborhood, paint, sell
lemonade or muffins to the neighbors.
Her home was a hotbed of creativity.

   And then as I got a little older,
I met Elaine Gauntt. She was the
mother of my best friend, Stacy. The
thing I remember most about Elaine
is that she smiled. Probably the most
perennially cheerful person I've ever
met. When I think of Elaine, I see
her standing in her kitchen. She was
always making something for someone
because she had four children, and it

seemed a lot of the time, all of their friends were at their house too. I remember Elaine presenting me with a breakfast of pancakes and orange juice on my sixteenth birthday. My parents went on a work trip over my birthday, so I stayed at the Gauntts. After Elaine made me pancakes, she popped a candle on top. Thoughtful. Kind. Resourceful. Very motherly.

Finally, there was Phyllis Jones. Phyllis was the mother of my first boyfriend, Gary. Looking back, I see that Phyllis was instrumental in the development of my faith. She taught the women's Bible studies at the church we attended, and though my mom went weekly to her Bible study, I never did.

Phyllis taught me about God through the context of her home and in the context of relationship. With her son, of course, but even more in their family. She took an interest in my spiritual development as a young woman. She was present as a spiritual model for motherhood, marriage, and what it looked like to serve family and community. I remember many impromptu conversations sitting on her sofa in her living room about God. I remember small Scripture cards on her kitchen table. Everywhere you turned at the Joneses, there was Jesus.

I am deeply grateful for these women. They were willing to be surrogate mothers, using their homes and pouring into me when I needed it. I think of them as organic mentors. We didn't sit down and complete a Bible study or even have an intentional meeting like I do now with Janet. But what these women all have in common is that they were soul tend-ers.

Who are the women in your life that currently tend to your soul? Who are your organic mentors? I hope you had a half-dozen women come to mind. But most of us only have one or two.

If you are in a season of feeling like there is no one watching over the care of your soul except you, then I would encourage you to pray and ask God for help. Research spiritual directors who live in your town, like I did. Or how about this: get thy butt to church and hang out there. I just know that there are some godly women around who would love to help you hear from God.

And can I just say something to my half-century sisters? Look around for some younger women, those dear daughters, who need a listening ear. And be just that. I have always said asking a simple question is one of the best ways I know to disciple others. You don't need a seminary degree. You've already got wisdom to share. Just be curious, listen for God and encourage the dear daughters in your life.

Jen Wilkins says, "Every believing woman who grows to maturity becomes, in her time, a spiritual mother to those following behind, whether she ever becomes a mom in physical terms. She fulfills that most basic calling of motherhood: nurturing the helpless and weak to maturity and strength."[22]

If we could only see the world

around us more like family, I think we'd have more women step up and act like mothers. I think we'd be less intimidated by aging and more interested in engaging with the younger women around us.

The women I've mentioned have or are contributing to my spiritual DNA. In their lives, I see things I'd like to duplicate. Who are the women in your life whose spiritual DNA you'd like to duplicate? No, I don't mean the spiritual superstars you follow on social media. I mean the women right where you live in your own community. Where are they? Who are they?

And as you look around your life for mentors realize you, too, are being a mentor to someone a few steps behind. So you are in the process of offering soul care to someone whether you realize it or not. It may feel small, but it's not. Your presence matters. Your kindness is important.

dear daughters

Susie Davis

Chapter Ten:

On Your One Beautiful Life

Chapter Ten:
On Your One Beautiful Life

I love you, God. I trust you. Thank you for my one beautiful life. Amen.

I see the house wren just outside the patio window. A plain brown bird, she is small and unexceptional. She looks at me with a sideways glance, as if she might want to come inside. The wavy geranium leaf stands above her like a large green umbrella, protecting her while she nudges the soil looking for insects.

This is what it feels like to be fifty years old. Not strong or powerful but light—like a bird. My feelings flutter endlessly poking around at my sense of self and my purpose in life.

Some days I wake with a longing for my twenties again. Wishing for a tight tummy and a curly-headed baby on my hip. I wish back for the days of

picture storybooks, baskets of blocks
sitting cozy in the corner, and apple
juice sippy cups spotting the kitchen
counter. Or my thirties, when I was
confident I could do it all. Raising
school-aged children while balancing
a part-time teaching job. The calendar
filled with after-school gymnastics,
hours of homework, and squeezing in
those highly coveted family dinners.
In my forties, I thought I really knew
things, like I somehow owned wisdom.
Marriage—check. Children—check.
Ministry—check.

I examined my experiences, tilted
them toward Scripture and based my
wisdom on the things that worked
right. And though I thought I was
getting "old" in my forties—I felt
fit and wonderful. My body never
complained. But my fifties gently
question, like the plain brown bird
looking back at me.

I sip my coffee, watching the
dappled light steal through cracks
in the picket fence and dance across
my small backyard. I wonder at my

birdlike thoughts. There are days I feel like sending out an SOS.

I am done raising my children. If all you ever wanted to be was a mother, it is hard to see it come to an end. I don't know how to be in this season of my life. I feel achy and hungry in the hollow of my soul. The emptiness scares me sometimes. I sang that mothering song nearly thirty years long, and now I've sung what feels like the final refrain.

In my professional life, things were ridiculously varied. Every time an opportunity presented itself, I gladly stepped forward like I was being called up for some grade school award. I taught drama for ten years. I was on the radio. I wrote books. And then, co-founding a church—that is still a work in progress. But every time God kicked open a door vocationally, I walked through the threshold. The different jobs proved exciting, fulfilling, and always challenging. I accomplished much of what I've hoped for even if I'm sitting here somewhat curious about where all the energy came from and if, in the end, what I did was even vaguely important to me or the people I love most in the world.

The wren sings a sweet, complex song. Beak wide open, her voice rises and falls in a simple elegance. Her little body quivers when she sings. It's evident she is giving everything only to the song. I see a faint ring of delicate white surrounding her small black eyes; she turns and blinks at me.

Maybe I didn't need to do so much when I was younger. All the outside jobs felt right at the time, even necessary for our budget. But in this current season, the temporary reward that accompanied the work feels insignificant now. Maybe there is no reason at all for experiences that build a resume. A mother doesn't need a resume.

I immediately think of Mimi. She is eighty-four years old. She is a beautifully content woman. I am lucky she is my mother. I've never once heard her wonder what she's supposed

to be doing with her life. She's never
worried about "making an impact" or
"leaving a legacy." And Mimi doesn't
stare in her mirror, hoping to blink
away the wrinkles. She hasn't plumped
up her forehead or tucked in her
chin. Instead, she told me in absolute
astonishment, she can't believe how
good she looks for her age. I can see
her now, her mousy brunette hair
tucked neatly behind her pearl studded
ears, she looks up and smiles at me and
then looks at her hands.

Recently, Mimi and I had a fancy
late lunch at Clark's on Sixth Street
with wine and fries and key lime pie. I
loved seeing her beautiful hands pick
up the spoon and let it sink carefully
into the meringue. She was slow and
deliberate about the key lime pie,
savoring each bite. Mimi is never
in a rush.

I can still see her hands patiently
turning the pages of a book
when I was young or
thoughtfully rolling
out pie dough at

*A*re you at ease in this season of your life? Do you find peace for your circumstances even when things are not the way you expected they would be? Because I think that is the secret to loving your one beautiful life.

holidays, and I well remember the way those hands soothed and patted all my babies. I am most grateful for those memories. And I am exceedingly thankful for her ever-peaceful presence in my life.

Mimi loves her one beautiful life. She is the one person in my life that I can truly say is continually content. Has her life been perfect? Of course not. Did she experience disappointment? I'm sure she has, but I can say from firsthand experience that she is the most deeply settled person I've ever met.

When I am with her, I wonder if I should be more at peace. Friendlier toward the obvious aging I'm experiencing? Slower and more deliberate about enjoying each season of my life? Should I be more like Mimi? Should you be more like Mimi? What are the things roughing up your soul? How do you seek to soothe them?

I think of one of my favorite counselors, Thomas Watson. No

matter that he is now a longtime resident in heaven. His words calm and settle me in the most profound way. When I am lost, I often find myself feeding on the words he wrote in his small book, *The Art of Divine Contentment*:

> *A contented Christian, being sweetly captivated under the authority of the Word, desires to be wholly at God's disposal, and is willing to live in that sphere and climate where God has set him.*[23]

Yes, that is Mimi. Always sweetly captivated in the sphere and climate God has set.

When she had to teach school to help make the house payment, and I tortured her with guilt over not packing my lunch in a brown paper bag personalized with curlicues, she never complained. She just got up earlier to pack my lunch and sign the paper bag, appeasing my childlike appetite for attention.

When I graduated from high school,
the last of her three children, there was
no overt sadness for the new season.
She watched happily as I walked the
long aisle at graduation. She gladly
bought all the necessities to build my
new nest in the dorm at Baylor. I'm
sure her big house felt empty the first
Monday morning I wasn't there at
breakfast, but she wasn't constantly
reaching out to me, hoping I'd come
back. She let me fly.

And then when the first great
grandchild was placed in her arms
seven short years ago, she smiled
contently. No remorse over all the
years now passed that managed to
make her a great grandma. No wishing
back.

Now in her eighties, she doesn't
mourn the loss of energy that keeps
her from rolling out dough for her
famous pumpkin pies at Thanksgiving.
There is no care spent lamenting
the fact that her age keeps her from
babysitting all the great grandbabies.
She is at ease in her life.

What about you? Are you at ease in this season of your life? Do you find peace for your circumstances even when things are not the way you expected they would be? Because I think that is the secret to loving your one beautiful life. It's in finding contentment, right here, right now.

The wren out my window has moved. She's sitting under the bronzed leaf of an autumn fern. Her tiny upright tail swishes.

I turn my thoughts to God.

I feel lost, God. Small and insignificant. I look back and wish for the days when I felt important and needed by my people. I miss my babies. And I look forward but can't see ahead. I don't know my place. I fight for contentment. Struggle for peace. I feel like a plain, ordinary bird in a big wide world of beautiful birds. Why does ordinary look beautiful on others but not on me? Why can't I be content to be an ordinary bird? Our songs intermingle

and mine drifts upward, lost in all
the voices. I know I am significant
to you. But every single feeling I
have tells me I'm irrelevant and
unimportant. Help me learn to be
content with this season in my life.
Teach me the secrets of contentment.

My feelings whimper around inside
my prayers, avoiding the truth I own.
I am glad God doesn't mind listening.
Grateful he offers to let me sit and flit
honestly in his presence.

There are so many seasons of change
in a woman's life from college to
career to marriage to mothering to un-
mothering. I haven't seen a season in
my life yet that didn't arrive dragging
along a lot of big feelings. And big
feelings like to show up and flip off all
the lights and make things difficult to
see.

I read somewhere that wrens can't
see in the dark. It only makes sense
then that they settle into their nests at
night and stay close to their home.

So maybe the reminder for us is this:

When we can't navigate the world for the darkness, we stay close to home. God is home. Feelings sometimes stand tall, intimidating a sense of self and purpose in any number of transitions or seasons. And this is precisely the time to stay home, close to God. Content with whatever is the sphere and climate. In these words, I am preaching to myself.

I want to be more like Mimi. Do you want to be more like Mimi too? Let's hand over our tired, unsettled hearts to God. Let's stay home until we see the light. Because night never stays forever. Morning will come.

And let's make this our prayer: I love you, God. I trust you. Thank you for my one beautiful life. Amen.

Susie Davis

....

....

....

....

....

....

....

....

....

....

....

....

dear daughters

Susie Davis

....

....

....

....

....

....

....

....

....

....

....

....

....

....

Notes

Introduction

[1] Ephesians 2:10 (NLT)
For we are God's masterpiece. He has created us anew in Christ Jesus, so we can do the good things he planned for us long ago.

[2] Ephesians 3:2 (NLT)
Assuming, by the way, that you know God gave me the special responsibility of extending his grace to you Gentiles.

[3] Ephesians 3:16 (NIV)
I pray that out of his glorious riches he may strengthen you with power through his Spirit in your inner being.

Chapter Two: On Life's Purpose

[4] Colossians 1:16 (NIV)
For in him all things were created: things in heaven and on earth, visible and invisible, whether thrones or powers or rulers or authorities; all things have been created through him and for him.

[5] Richard J. Foster, *Prayers from the Heart* (HarperOne, 1994) xi.

[6] Proverbs 31:18 (NASB)
She senses that her gain is good;
Her lamp does not go out at night.

[7] Colossians 1:9 (NLT)
So we have not stopped praying for you since we first heard about you. We ask God to give you complete knowledge of his will and to give you spiritual wisdom and understanding.

Chapter Three: On Loving Your Body

[8] Shauna Niequist, *Bread and Wine: A Love Letter to Life Around the Table with Recipes* (Zondervan, 2013) 36.

[9] Nora Ephron, *I Feel Bad About My Neck: And Other Thoughts on Being a Woman* (Knopf, 2006) 124.

[10] Carrie Underwood, "We're Young and Beautiful," track 10 on *Some Hearts* (Arista, 2005).

Chapter Four: On Your Relationship with Your Father

[11] 2 Corinthians 1:3 (NIV)
Praise be to the God and Father of our Lord Jesus Christ, the Father of compassion and the God of all comfort.

[12] Isaiah 40:29 (NIV)
He gives strength to the weary
  and increases the power of the weak.

[13] Psalm 139:1-6 (ESV)
O Lord, you have searched me and known me!
You know when I sit down and when I rise up;
  you discern my thoughts from afar.

You search out my path and my lying down
    and are acquainted with all my ways.
Even before a word is on my tongue,
    behold, O LORD, you know it altogether.
You hem me in, behind and before,
    and lay your hand upon me.
Such knowledge is too wonderful for me;
    it is high; I cannot attain it.

Chapter Six: On Feeling Small

[14] Brother Lawrence, *The Practice of the Presence of God with Spiritual Maxims* (Revell, 1967), 90-91.

[15] Oswald Chambers, *My Utmost for His Highest* (Dodd, Mead & Co, 1935) 327.

Chapter Seven: On Transitions

[16] Mark 12:30 (NIV)
Love the Lord your God with all your heart and with all your soul and with all your mind and with all your strength.

[17] John Eldredge, *Waking the Dead* (Nelson Books, 2016) 55.

[18] Proverbs 4:23 NLT
Guard your heart above all else,
    for it determines the course of your life.

[19] Eldredge, *Waking the Dead*, 25.

Notes

Chapter Eight: On Living Wholeheartedly

[20] David Whyte, "Sweet Darkness" https://onbeing.org/blog/sweet-darkness/.

Chapter Nine: On Finding Care for Your Soul

[21] Sophie Hudson, *Giddy Up Eunice* (B&H Books, 2016) 41.

[22] Jen Wilkin, https://www.ligonier.org/learn/articles/mothers-church/.

Chapter Ten: On Your One Beautiful Life

[23] Thomas Watson, *The Art of Divine Contentment* (Soli Deo Gloria Publications, 2001) 109.

Acknowledgments

Emily, Amy, and Sara—For being my own dear daughters. For letting me ask hard questions, play wildly and for grace when I disappoint you. I pray God will help me to be the kind of woman that inspires you to love God with all your energy, all of your one beautiful life.

Linda Stafford—You've always been a few steps ahead. Thank you for showing me where to put my feet, for holding my heart when I was vulnerable and for making me laugh endlessly (even in inappropriate situations). You are the best sister a girl could ever ask for, and I am indebted for your love and care of me and my people.

Esther Fedorkevich—I guess I should start by thanking Randy Phillips for inviting us to lunch because from there, it's been one book after another. Thank you for your representation, your advocacy, and your friendship. The Fedd Agency is a place full of delightful professional people who love good words and Good News. I am grateful.

Whitney Gossett—Oh what a joy you are in my life. A champion of my creativity with a sure steady voice and an open glad heart. Thank you for time, your vision, and your energy. Your tenacity in finding this book a home will be a gift to dear daughters and spiritual mamas everywhere.

Lauren Hall—You are a treasure. Thank you for your encouragement to stand steady and be me in a world that sometimes seems full of crazy. Thank you for long meetings with coffee and candles. Thank you for pizza, red wine, and deep questions.

Acknowledgments

Karen Longino—Thank you for your enthusiasm and your warm welcome. Your passion for dear daughters and spiritual mamas is evident in the home you created for this message. My heart is full because of you.

Bailey Greenlees—How grateful I am you said yes to transitions and showed up in my space to manage all things ministry, home, and life. You are a blessing, and I am humbled to have you by my side.

Dr. Andrew Forrester—My nephew, my friend, my editor. Thank you for reading all the chapters, gently asking questions, and pointing out where things could be better. You made the process easy and fun.

Chloe Hamaker—Thank you for the most beautiful design for this book cover. You are the best at sorting through all my ideas and coming up with things that sing. Thank you for sharing your effervescence with me and my projects.

Will Davis Jr.—To the man who listens to all my early morning ideas, brings me coffee, and encourages me to fulfill the ministry God called me to, whatever that may be. I love you.